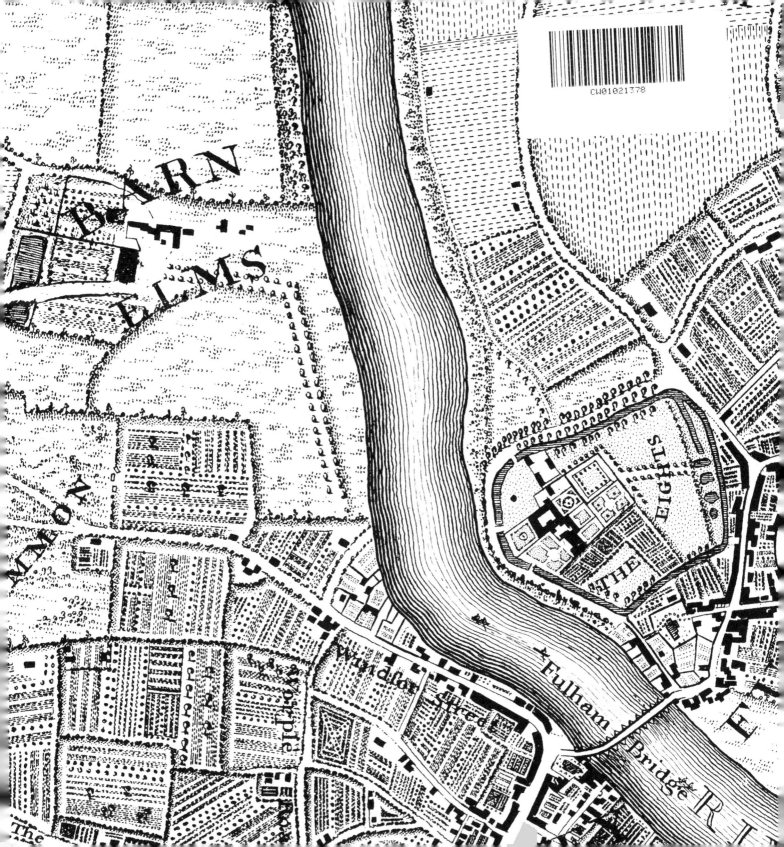

BARN
ELMS

MMON

THE EIGHTS

Windsor Street

Fulham Bridge

The

WILD ABOUT
Barnes

THE VILLAGE ON THE RIVER

By Andrew Wilson

Historian: Maisie Brown

Kindly supported by

Winkworth

To my lovely wife, Diana, my number one supporter.

Clockwise from top left: Barnes Terrace, Barnes Bridge, Barnes Green and Barnes Pond

Foreword

A great city is really a collection of urban villages, each with its own identity contributing to the overall charm and character of the metropolis. Barnes is one of London's most attractive villages, a community which stretches across and around woods and common land from the station to the banks of the Thames.

Its streets are lined by some of the most attractive houses in any city; no wonder most people don't ever want to leave once they have put down their roots here. Moreover, our village community has all the urban attributes which have not yet been obliterated by the onward march of shopping malls.

The closing of Hammersmith Bridge makes us even more aware of the pleasure of living in our own part of what George Melly used to call transpontine London. The deplorable buck passing about repairing or replacing the bridge has one benefit alone which is to increase our understanding of how lucky we are to live in Barnes.

We have a great bookshop, staffed by people who love books and can tell you with authority what you should be reading. There are very good bakers and greengrocers. There's a terrific farmers' market every Saturday morning bringing fresh fish, great apples, seasonable vegetables, delicious onion tarts, bread and delicatessen treats to the spoilt-rotten residents.

There are busy churches and good pubs, including the Bull's Head where you can hear some of the best jazz in London over a pint. At the bottom of Castlenau we also have excellent restaurants representing the cuisine of all parts of the world including now Japan. There is the best Italian restaurant in the whole city. For dog-owners like me the walks are easy and many: from the home past the pond and the ducks to the best newsagent in London for the Sunday papers; across to the cemetery and the fields beyond: up to the river and the tow-path to Hammersmith Bridge. Alas the bird sanctuary at the Wetlands is no good for dogs but great for grand-children, especially if you buy a brownie for them in the café afterwards.

So, Barnes for me is not just where I sleep but where I live and want to live until closing time. I see no reason why it should ever change. *Semper eadem*, as the Chancellor of Oxford might put it.

Lord Patten of Barnes

Welcome to Wild About Barnes

Welcome to a brand new edition of what has been my most popular book to date, and what turned out to be the catalyst for the series of books that I have been steadily building over the past 10 years on the local area. I am indebted to Isla Dawes, who used to run Barnes Bookshop, who initially gave me the idea and to the way that Venetia and her team in Church Road have continued to support what I do. Living on the borders of Barnes, I feel I know this area really well, especially as I walk my dog on the common almost every day. But even I didn't know half the things that I discovered when originally putting this book together. A lot has changed in the last 10 years, not all of it good either, Hammersmith Bridge has had to be closed, which has caused no end of trouble for everyone. Then of course we have had to deal with the pandemic, which has been devastating for business and people alike. However, we are an enterprising lot in

Barnes and it's a testament to our resilience that our high street is fighting back and its great to see many new shops popping up.

My original book took over a year to produce and with the added incentive of an annual calendar to publish, which I first produced back in 2014, I have had plenty of opportunities to take many new pictures. So, besides an update to some of the text, I have also changed almost all of the imagery. Ably assisted by Helen and David Deaton from the Barnes & Mortlake History Society, I am also really pleased to say that we have had great fun placing a few older pictures, which together with my new ones shows us just how things have changed through the years. Other than this, my book is very much as before, a wonderful catalogue of just how lovely our local area is. As with some of my other books, I have included a simple map to help you place my pictures geographically and I am grateful to my brother, Jeremy Wilson, for his help producing this. With my new books I have been introducing local walks but with

Barnes we have the original, The Barnes Trail, which my brother also helped with. So please don't take my word for it, discover Barnes for yourself, with all revealed on page 72.

As with all of my books, it is never a one man show and there are numerous people to thank. Up first, Maisie Brown, for supplying not only an introduction but also a lot of the captions. To Lord Patten, for providing such a wonderfully evocative foreword, which he has kindly updated for 2021. I would also like to thank Gyles Brandreth, Isla Blair, Julian Glover and Patricia Hodge for taking time out of their busy schedules to give me a few lines on why they love Barnes so much and their contributions can be found spread out over the pages. They may now be 10 years old but haven't they stood the test of time. May I also thank all the people whose 'property' I visited to take pictures, from Richmond Council who own much of it to the owners of Milbourne House in Station Road, the oldest house in Barnes, who very kindly invited me in to take a picture. Finally, to Simon Banks and all the staff at Charles Banks, one of local estate agents, who kindly sponsored the first edition and got me started. There is never enough space to thank everybody and please forgive me if I have inadvertently forgotten to mention you. I love this area and I hope that a little of this passion leaps off the pages as you glance through my latest photography.

Left: Josie, my springer spaniel and constant companion on the river at low tide

Andrew Wilson and Josie
August 2021

For up to date news on all things Barnes, please be sure to subscribe to The Barnes Village Bugle, produced by local resident Sarah Arthur **www.barnesvillagebugle.co.uk**

Contents

A Short History of the Area	6	Barnes in Bloom	98	**Barnes Common**	**150**
The Pond & The Green	10	Ferry Road	100	*and other open spaces*	
Winter	12	The High Street	101	Winter	152
Spring & Summer	20	Barnes in Lockdown	106	Spring	156
Barnes Fair	28	Rocks Lane	108	Green, Blue & Gold	158
Autumn	30	Station Road & Barnes Station	110	Long Hot Days of Summer	162
The Lion Houses	36	White Hart Lane & West Barnes	114	Down by the Brook	164
The River & The Terrace	**38**	Ye White Hart	116	Bringing in the Hay	165
Rowing & The Boat Race	56	Westfield Allotments	120	It's a Small World	166
Barnes Bridge	**60**	Vine Road Recreation Ground	121	Autumn	168
Barnes at Christmas	70	Hidden Barnes	122	Leg o' Mutton Nature Reserve	174
Barnes Trail	72	**North Barnes**	**124**	Barn Elms	182
Street Scenes	**74**	Hammersmith Bridge	136	The Old Cemetery	183
Church Road	76	Harrods Village & Barnes Waterside	140	WWT London Wetland Centre	184
Farmers' Market	80	St Paul's School & Colet Court	142		
The Parish Church of St Mary, Barnes	88	Harrodian School	146		

Barnes

A SHORT HISTORY OF THE AREA
by Maisie Brown

Barnes is a small suburb of south-west London, lying on the south bank of the Thames, some six miles distant from Hyde Park Corner. The greater part of the land is a peninsula, bordered on three sides by a pronounced northern meander of the Thames. The terrain is almost uniformly flat, rising only 27ft above flood level at Mill Hill on Barnes Common. Barnes was once in the County of Surrey. On April 1st 1965 it became part of the Greater London Borough of Richmond upon Thames.

Long before the Norman Conquest in 1066, Barnes was a settled village within the Archbishop of Canterbury's Manor of Mortlake in the county of Surrey, together with Putney, Roehampton, Wimbledon and Mortlake itself. Early in the reign of the Anglo Saxon King Athelstan (925–939 AD), Barnes became a separate manor held in Lordship by the Dean and Chapter of St. Paul's Cathedral, London. It was one of eighteen small manors within easy reach of London owned by the Cathedral Chapter and known collectively as the Communa. "The revenue and produce of which were appropriated to the support and sustenance of all members of the Cathedral in regular gradation...from the Dean down to the humblest servitor – the doorkeeper

of the brewery." The manors were leased to a Firmarius, an office limited to resident canons which was a source of wealth. They in turn sub-let the manors to tenants who tended the soil and were required to send regular quantities of grain to the Cathedral – wheat, oats and barley – to make bread and beer. Most of the eighteen manors were in Middlesex; Barnes was the only one on the Surrey bank of the Thames.

In the Great Survey of England, ordered by William I in 1086, better known as the Domesday Book, Barnes is recorded as a settled pre-conquest Anglo Saxon village, "the land of St. Paul's, London", held by the Canons of St. Paul's. In 1086 the population numbered around 60 to 65. The manor appears to have been close to what used to be termed the 'classic manor', made up of land reserved for the lord of the manor, known as the demesne with the remainder shared equally among the village tenants. In Barnes the demesne amounted to 460 acres to the north of the village, later known as the Barn Elms Estate. The tenants shared the two arable fields, the Westfield and the Northfield, in equal lots, plus a limited amount of meadow for animal winter feed. In return they were obliged to work for three days in each week on the demesne plus payments in money or kind. No mention is made of the "waste" or Common, an invaluable resource for the tenants providing forage for their geese and pigs and fallen wood for fuel, but was probably considered not

Below: Barnes Parish Church, 1837 (from a lithography by Laura Jones) – Barnes & Mortlake History Society

worth a mention by the Norman assessors as it was worth very little to the exchequer.

By the end of the 15th century, payment in kind had been commuted into money payment in Barnes. And in 1467, Sir John Saye, Chancellor to Edward IV, became the first of a long line of lay tenants who leased the Barn Elms Estate and possibly built the first Manor House, Barn Elms, in its grounds.

In 1579 Elizabeth I leased the Manor of Barnes and gave it to her spymaster-in-chief, Sir Francis Walsingham, who was there until his death in 1590. During his tenure the Queen is known to have visited Barn Elms on several occasions sometimes alone and at other times with her court. Living nearby at Milbourne House (see page 113), was Robert Beale, secretary to Sir Francis and no doubt the vexed question of what to do about Mary, Queen of Scots was often discussed at Barn Elms. Beale was among the party who carried the order to Fotheringay for the execution of the unfortunate Queen and witnessed her beheading.

Walsingham, head of a network of domestic and foreign spies, probably appreciated the seclusion of the estate, accessible only by river and remote from the village which, due to the lack of a permanent river crossing, was itself a quiet and isolated place. However, the river Thames was a major highway carrying both goods and people, so that isolation was never total.

At the beginning of the 17th century, the pattern of open field farming in the Westfield and Northfield, laid down centuries before, was rapidly transformed into one of small individual enclosures. As peasant farmers responded to the demands of the growing London fruit and vegetable market they turned from cereal crops to market gardening. Each day river barges carrying garden produce were seen leaving Barnes bound for the newly opened Covent Garden Market. Civil War, when it came, left the market gardens undisturbed as no battles were fought in Barnes. It was the gardeners pockets which suffered. Between 1642 and 1645 heavy taxation imposed by the Parliamentarians, the commandeering of horses and food supplies and the billeting of soldiers on private households weighed heavily on all but the poorest in Barnes.

Towards the end of the century a period of slow recovery which began with the restoration of the Monarchy began to gather pace and the village entered into a period of mild prosperity. The population increased, as did the number of small traders and craftsmen. Shops and inns opened on the path between the two open fields, which was now known as 'the Streete'. Barnes even had its own 'garden centre' where William Blinde stocked rare plants, still relatively new to England, as well as the 'ordinarie sortes of flowers'.

All this was largely due to the market garden trade with London. The market

Below: Painting of the Terrace from 1896 by S. Key. Thank you to the Barnes & Mortlake History Society for the use of this image.

gardens were the backbone of the local economy in Barnes for the next 230 years. The last market gardener left in 1926.

When the first census was taken in 1801, Barnes had a population of 860. The 1838 Tithe Map of Barnes recorded a landscape consisting mostly of market gardens, farms and common land. The Manor House was at Barn Elms, there were a number of large houses along The Terrace and others stood in their own grounds around The Green and along Church Road. Some were leased as summer lets or for longer periods by well-to-do Londoners escaping from the unhealthy city. They contrasted sharply with the huddle of mean cottages crammed into the courts and alleys behind the High Street and The Terrace which housed the 'working classes', mostly migrants who came to work in the market gardens. One visitor described the cottages as closely resembling overcrowded pigsties.

For many years, wealthy families such as the merchant bankers, like the Hoares, who leased the Barn Elms estate from 1732 to 1824, favoured Barnes as a semi-rural retreat, conveniently within reach

of their businesses in the City of London, and were content to preserve their peaceful surroundings by sub-letting their surplus land to market gardeners and farmers. When the suggestion of a bridge joining Hammersmith to Barnes was first raised in parliament in 1671 it had been greeted by laughter and cries of "why build a bridge to a place where nobody lives."

A proposal in 1817 by the newly formed Hammersmith Bridge Company to build a bridge providing the most direct way from London to the South West was taken more seriously.

A Bill authorising the building of the bridge, had little chance of being enacted in Parliament until the land for an approach road had been acquired and the only possible route was through the Barn Elms estate. Henry Hugh Hoare the lessee, was adamant. If the company wanted to build their road across his land they would have to buy the lease of the entire estate, which eventually they did, for £35,000. The enabling Bill was enacted on 9th June 1824 and the first Hammersmith Bridge designed by William Tierney Clark was opened on 6th October 1827 (pictured left). It was the first of the major changes destined to transform a quiet village into a suburb of London. The next was the coming of the railway in 1846, since when Barnes has slowly developed into the pleasant leafy place we know today.

Maisie Brown
Past chair of the Barnes & Mortlake History Society and the author of several books on the local area including *Barnes and Mortlake Past*.

Top: A painting of The Limes (now 123 Mortlake High Street) by JMW Turner in 1827. The house was built in 1720 as council offices, it was damaged by bombs in 1940 and after restoration the house is still used as commercial offices.

THE OXFORD AND CAMBRIDGE UNIVERSITY BOAT-RACE ON SATURDAY LAST: SCENE AT HAMMERSMITH BRIDGE—SEE PAGE 231.

Bottom: The first Hammersmith Bridge, depicting the Boat Race and spectators literally hanging off the bridge.

Barnes

This watercolour map, which has been produced especially for this publication is not meant to be to scale but purely to act as a guide to Barnes and some of the places covered by this book.

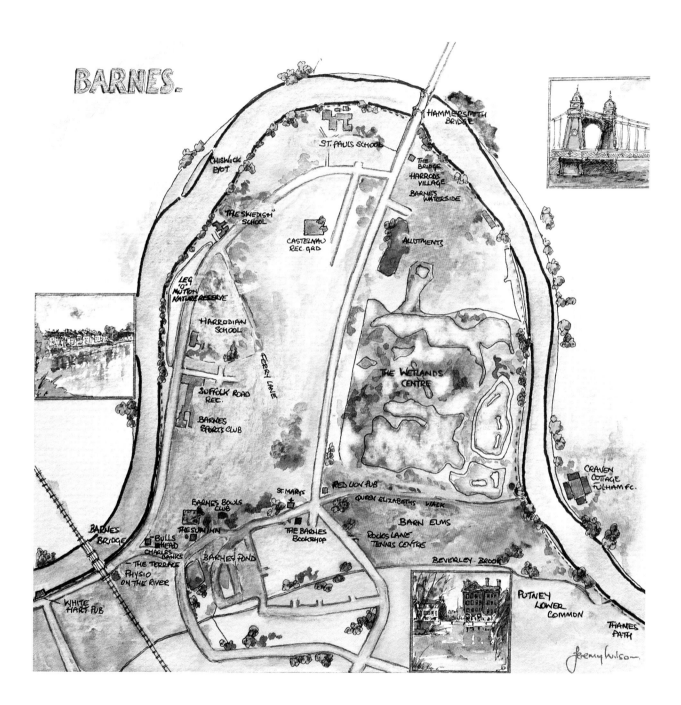

BARNES.

HAMMERSMITH BRIDGE

ST. PAULS SCHOOL

CHISWICK EYOT

THE BRIDGE

HARRODS VILLAGE

BARNES WATERSIDE

THE SWEDISH SCHOOL

CASTELNAU REC. GRD

ALLOTMENTS

LEG "O" MUTTON NATURE RESERVE

HARRODIAN SCHOOL

FERRY LANE

THE WETLANDS CENTRE

SUFFOLK ROAD REC.

BARNES SPORTS CLUB

CRAVEN COTTAGE FULHAM F.C.

RED LION PUB

ST. MARYS

QUEEN ELIZABETHS WALK

BARNES BOWLS CLUB

BARN ELMS

ROCKS LANE TENNIS CENTRE

THE SUN INN

BARNES BRIDGE

BULLS HEAD

THE BARNES BOOKSHOP

CHARLES BANKS

BEVERLEY BROOK

THE TERRACE

BARNES POND

PUTNEY LOWER COMMON

PHYSIO ON THE RIVER

WHITE HART PUB

THAMES PATH

Jeremy Wilson

9

The Pond & The Green

The pond on Barnes Green has long been the community focal point of Barnes Village. Known to generations of children as a place to feed the ducks and to Barnes people in general as somewhere to spare a moment to sit and watch the world go by. Just how long the pond has been there, nobody knows. Archival references are rare, one being a survey of the manor of Barnes in 1649, when it was named as The Great Pond, part of the glebe land belonging to the Rector of St. Mary's Parish Church, although its origins are thought to date back far earlier than the 17th Century. Also mentioned in the survey were three smaller ponds on the Green. They lasted until the 19th Century, during which they were drained at various times due to stagnation.

A serious threat to the pond came in 1824, when the Hammersmith Bridge Company published a plan to run a road across its centre as part of an approach road to their proposed bridge across the Thames. Thankfully the plan was abandoned. In April, 2001, early morning walkers on the green were the first to be greeted by the amazing sight of the pond minus its water. No definitive cause was ever established. The local community, led by the Barnes Community Association together with Richmond Council, raised a substantial amount of money that enabled the pond to be 'repaired'; fitting for the first time in its long history with an artificial liner.

Winter

It doesn't often snow in Barnes, so you have to be quick. Pictures taken early in 2021.

The Pond is transformed when it's cold enough for some ice. Sadly, this can sometimes coincide with our resident family of Egyptian geese having their young. They are good parents and if the weather and predators, like the heron, are kind to them, they can survive. There is no lack of locals ready to feed them.

Spring & Summer

The crocuses, along with some snowdrops are the first things to appear on the green, sometimes even as early as late December. They make a magnificent display come February.

Opposite: Always a popular feature of village life, our resident pair of swans had another 7 goslings this year (late April 2021). It is strange to note that this seems to be a regular thing for them, discounting 2020, they had seven in 2019, 2017 and 2016).

Opposite, Bottom Left:
Barnes Methodist Church

Opposite, Bottom Right: This square box-like structure on the side of Beverley Brook by the bridge to the common was placed there in 1960. It housed a pump which sent water from the brook to the pond via an underground pipe across the Green. By the early 1970s the pipe was found to be ineffective, since then no water from the brook has entered the pond.

Bottom Left: Lisa from the OSO, the theatre on the green, and one of our Barnes Heroes (please see page 87 for the full story on our heroes).

Bottom Right: The green flooding is clearly a regular occurrence, as well as this wonderful picture from The Barnes & Mortlake Historical Society depicting a flood from over 100 years ago (bottom right), here are some more recent ones from the last 5 years.

THE POND BARNES

Johns 6358

23

Opposite, Bottom Left: This pencil drawing of the pond as it used to be, is the same scene as appears left. Thank you to the Barnes & Mortlake History Society for the use of this picture.

Opposite, Bottom Right: The Egyptian geese always like to take up a prominent high position when protecting their young.

This Page, Bottom Right: The view of the pond looking back from a window in the big red building.

"Ah! Barnes. For me it was love at first sight. Green and leafy, with low-rise houses, a flowing waterside and a wetland centre, a vast common, a brook, a duck pond, and a quaintness that's the nearest approximation to the Lincolnshire villages of my childhood yet within 20 minutes of Piccadilly Circus (if you erase the traffic)... The perfect hybrid between London and the country. After 36 years here, I think one could say the love affair is enduring".

PATRICIA HODGE – ACTRESS OCT 2011

Barnes Fair

Always a highlight of the village calendar, the annual Barnes Fair on the second Saturday of July (organised so brilliantly by The Barnes Community Association) was again, like in 2020, a casualty of the Covid Pandemic in 2021. These pictures are a selection from some earlier events, can you spot yourself?

Autumn

The Green in autumn can be a beautiful time of year.

Even moving out from the green to the surrounding streets, there is still autumnal beauty to be found on local roads

This Page, Top:
Woodlands Road.

Bottom Left:
Two peas in a pod.

Bottom Right:
Glebe Road.

Opposite, Top Left:
The Terrace.

Opposite, Top Right:
Parke Road.

Opposite, Bottom:
Suffolk Road Recreation Ground.

The Lion Houses

The Lion Houses are a major feature of the homes that surround the Green and were built by a local builder, James or Jimmy Nicholls, between 1899 and 1903. Nicholls' building yard was at the end of Willow Avenue, known as Beverley Works. The first to be built were Nos. 1 to 14 The Crescent, followed by others in Laurel Road (top below), Hillersdon Avenue and Glebe Road (opposite page). An attractive and unusual feature of the houses, much prized by their owners, is the small sandstone lions that peer down at passers-by from every vantage point. It is said that their widespread use was due to 1,000 lions being supplied by mistake for the 100 ordered by the builder.

So popular, that some people like to place them whatever the setting (Archway Street, West Barnes, bottom left).

The River & The Terrace

The Terrace is a row of highly individual riverside dwellings, mostly residential, running west from the end of Barnes High Street to White Hart Lane. The larger houses mostly date from the early to mid-18th Century. Some of the smaller houses that are thought to have started out as watermens' cottages, may be considerably older, possibly dating from the 16th century. They would have been among the earliest buildings to appear on the riverside boundary of the Westfield, one of the two medieval open fields of Barnes. During the 18th and 19th century the larger houses were popular as summer lets, especially to wealthy Londoners making their escape from the overcrowded and unhealthy city.

Some houses no longer exist. Several made way for Barnes Railway Bridge in 1849, its widening in 1895 and for Barnes Bridge Station in 1916. And slightly further to the west the largest and most imposing house on The Terrace, Elm Bank, lost five acres of its land to Elm Bank Gardens in 1896. The house itself disappeared to make way for Elm Bank Mansions built in 1906 (see picture below). Only the entrance to the carriage driveway, marked by two decorative pillars, and the Tower, a folly which stood in its grounds, still stands, the latter as part of Tower House (see picture below). River House, an apartment block, was built in 1963 on the former site of Nos 18–24. More recently, a prominent feature of The Terrace, a malt house dating from the 18th Century, was demolished to make way for Numbers 1–4 Maltings Close, a residential development which somewhat surprisingly stands with its back to the riverside view. But happily several old houses and cottages still stand, looking outwardly much the same as in old prints of The Terrace and lending a touch of bygone elegance to the riverside scene. (See page 7 for a painting from 1896 depicting the Terrace as the artist perceived it then).

Riverside Mansions and Tower House, which has recently undergone some major refurbishment outside and in and looks impressive.

"I moved to Barnes in 1968 and cannot imagine living anywhere else. It is the last remaining 'village' in London with a wonderful community spirit. There are many and varied societies and organisations and I shop locally, not just in support, but because the local shops are so good. There is a thriving WI, Farmer's Market and a vibrant Literary Society and Music and Drama Society. I travel a great deal but each time a cross Hammersmith Bridge I sigh and say – Ah, Barnes – because coming home here is the best feeling one could have."

ISLA BLAIR, NOVELIST 2011

Sadly, since Isla kindly supplied this splendid quote, and as we go to press (Summer 2021) we have been deprived of the use of Hammersmith Bridge for over 18 months, although it has just reopened to pedestrians and cyclists.

Overleaf: Sunrise over The Terrace

The Terrace has been home to some famous residents in its time. The most well known have been commemorated by the prestigious blue plaque, which are found across London. The Terrace was home to the composer, Gustav Holst and the founder of the Royal Ballet, Ninette de Valois.

Opposite, Top Left: The Terrace from the north side embankment, by the rowing club.

This Page, Top: The Wisteria on this house on the Terrace is always a highlight.

Bottom, Across Both Pages: In this wonderful selection of pictures, you can see how Barnes Bridge Station has changed over the years. It is now Physio-On-The-River, where my wife has her business. Thank you to Richmond Archives and The Barnes & Mortlake History Society for the use of these old pictures.

Left: The wonderful mural under Barnes Bridge is a new addition, commissioned by The BCA, it went up in the autumn of 2020.

The Terrace, Barnes.

Left: The Terrace as it used to look in the early 20th Century. Thank you to the Barnes & Mortlake History Society for the use of these pictures.

This Page: The Terrace as it used to look and today. Note the lack of any wall in the picture on the far left. Thank you to the Barnes & Mortlake History Society for the use of these pictures.

Opposite: The White Hart holding one of its regular barbecues; pre-covid, of course.

Top: This panoramic picture was taken from the roof of The Bull's Head.

A group of fishermen checking the fish stock in the river, on behalf of Defra following some pollution back in the summer of 2011.

Rowing & The Boat Race

The Head of the River Race: A timed race for eights, rowed annually on the Thames from Mortlake to Putney. The first Head of the River Race took place on the 12th December 1926 with 40 crews competing. Today the entry is limited to 420 crews, several being crews from abroad who are strongly advised to take a practice run on the extremely hazardous course before taking part in the race.

Opposite and This Page: The Boat Race in 2017. Sadly, the race didn't happen in 2020 and was held out of town in 2021 on account of Covid.

The Oxford and Cambridge Boat Race: The race was the brainchild of two student friends in 1829 – Charles Merivale at Cambridge and Charles Wordsworth at Oxford. The first race took place on 12th March 1829 at Henley. Oxford were clear winners after a restart. The first race held on the Thames from Putney to Mortlake was rowed in 1845 and from 1856, apart from the war years, it became an annual event. During the 19th century spectators, not one of whom were known to have fallen into the river, hung from every vantage point high on Hammersmith Bridge hoping for a glimpse of the passing eights (see page 8 for a painting that depicts this). Health and safety regulations prevent this happening today. The pictures on this page were taken at the 2011 Boat Race which Oxford won by four lengths.

Barnes Bridge

The original slender, three-span cast iron bridge (on the upstream side of the bridge) across the Thames designed by Joseph Locke, dates from the opening of the Hounslow loop line in 1849 (see page 65 for a painting of the original bridge). In 1895 it was replaced by the more workmanlike crossing seen today (see below for a picture of the new bridge under construction).

Designed by Edward Andrews for the London and South Western Railway Company its heavy wrought-iron bow string girders carrying two railway tracks across the river have caused it to be named by some as 'the ugliest bridge on the Thames'. I would tend to disagree with this sentiment, in fact I love it. Part of the original bridge survives unused on the up-stream side and the recent re-painting of the entire structure in two shades of grey, similar to the colours used on the 1849 bridge, have considerably improved its appearance. The bridge was listed as a Grade II structure in 1983.

"I am not sure that it's really a good idea to publish a book about the beauty of Barnes. Those of us who are lucky enough to live here don't necessarily want to spread the word. But perhaps it's too late. It seems that Barnes has had its admirers for centuries. Samuel Pepys loved Barnes. According to his diary, he used to wander across Barn Elms, watching the girls go by. Henry Fielding, the novelist and magistrate, loved Barnes. He lived here. (I think there should be a statue of him on the traffic island outside his house by Barnes Pond.)"

GYLES BRANDRETH – LOCAL RESIDENT, BROADCASTER, WRITER AND ALL ROUND GOOD EGG

Inset: Barnes Bridge c. 1849

This Page, Bottom Left: This is the old bridge as it is today and there is a group working locally to try and reopen it as a footbridge. It is slow work and quite an undertaking on account of the structure. I for one wish them every success, as it would be a fabulous addition to the local area and Covid really showed up the limitations, with social distancing, of the footbridge on the other side.

Barnes at Christmas

This Page, Clockwise from Top: Rose House 2020, Nassau Road, BCA Christmas Tree Church Road 2020 and three shots of the High Street with a little fake snow and some carols to jolly things along. **Opposite Page, Clockwise from Top Left:** Orange Pekoe, The Peach Tree Clinic, Madrid Road, an OSO Christmas 2020, Bobby & friends, Castelnau, Nina in Church Road and in the middle, Oh Darling in White Hart Lane.

The Barnes Trail

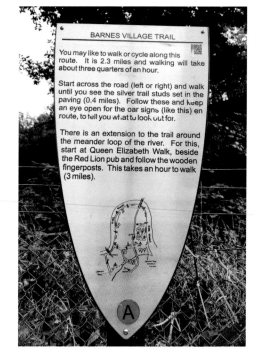

BARNES VILLAGE TRAIL

You may like to walk or cycle along this route. It is 2.3 miles and walking will take about three quarters of an hour.

Start across the road (left or right) and walk until you see the silver trail studs set in the paving (0.4 miles). Follow these and keep an eye open for the oar signs (like this) en route, to tell you what to look out for.

There is an extension to the trail around the meander loop of the river. For this, start at Queen Elizabeth Walk, beside the Red Lion pub and follow the wooden fingerposts. This takes an hour to walk (3 miles).

Barnes is a stunning village with many attractions and sites of interest. Visitors can find out more about this special village by walking the Barnes Trail. The 2.3 mile trail, and the 3 mile extension, have been designed to show Barnes at its best. The route is circular, so it doesn't matter where you start – just follow the silver 'Barnes Trail' discs set in the ground. If you walk quickly, you can complete the trail in under an hour – but why not take your time, soak up the surroundings, and enjoy the shops, cafés, pubs and restaurants as you go. Even better, use the trail as a starting point to explore more of Barnes.

Historical points of interest such as the riverside, the village pond and common and buildings such as the famous former Olympic recording studios are described on information plaques shaped like oars placed along the route. Four 'introductory' oars guide visitors at the main public transport locations. The oars feature QR codes for scanning with a smartphone or tablet to access additional information.

A map of the route with illustrations of key sites and buildings guides walkers around the trail. You can pick up a copy of the Barnes Trail map from Rose House, the home of the Barnes Community Association. This map will guide you around the trail and point out the historical sites of interest along the way.

The Barnes Trail has been funded by the Mayor of London's Outer London Fund and developed in association with the London Borough of Richmond upon Thames and the Barnes Community Association.

Emma Robinson
Barnes Town Centre Manager

BARNES
AND THE
BARNES TRAIL

LONSDALE ROAD

CASTELNAU A306

THE BRIDGE PUB

ALLOT

BOILEAU ROAD

LEG "O" MUTTON NATURE RESERVE

VERDUN ROAD

FERRY ROAD

MADRID ROAD

CASTELNAU A306

THE WETLANDS CENTRE

THE RED LIONAUF

QUEEN ELIZABETH WALK

BARN ELMS

BEVERLEY BROOK

CHURCH ROAD A3003

THE BULL'S HEAD

THE SUN INN

BARNES HIGH ST

THE COACH AND HORSES

BARNES BRIDGE ST

RIVER ROAD

RECTORY RD

RAILWAY SIDE

ROCK'S LANE

CEMETERY

PUTNEY LOWER COMMON

YE WHITE HART

THE ELM BANK GDNS

WHITE LADDER

CHARLES ST

RODNEY ST

WESTFIELD

KINGSLEY ST

LANVALE

THE IDLE HOUR

STATION ROAD

BEVERLEY

ELIZABETH ST

THE BROWN DOG

THE TREE HOUSE

RAILWAY SIDE

VINE ROAD

MILL MILL ROAD

RADNLAGH AV

BARNES

COMMON

BARNES ST

Jeremy Wilson

the Brown Dog

THE IDLE HOUR

73

Street Scenes

There are so many wonderful aspects of living and working in Barnes, one being the variety and sheer range of little shops that we have. The pandemic has of course made things very tough for the high street, but we have fared better than most, in no small way helped by our thriving local Community Association, based in Rose House in the High Street (see page 101). They see the importance of a thriving high street for everyone in the community and have employed a Town Centre Manager, Emma Robinson, for the last 8 years or so to help coordinate this, and fantastic she is too. Besides the High Street and Church Road, there are of course many other roads, mostly residential, that make up our community and too many to feature here but going alphabetically, I take a look at some.

The High Street as it was over 100 years ago.

Church Road

This Page and Overleaf: the start of Church Road by The Pond.

Above: The resident swans crossing the road with their small cygnets in tow, this is a regular and pleasant occurrence during early summer, when they cross to feed on the lush grass to be found on the island. After this continued to occur a sign was erected to warn drivers.

SLOW
Swans crossing..
or they might be geese but
you won't see a pelican crossing

The Farmers' Market

The Farmers' Market, in the car park of the Essex House doctors' surgery, was first started back in 1998 and was one of the first farmers markets in London. It was originally set up by a local businessman but was taken over in 2002 by Jamie Walker and Will Smith who both had stands already on the market (Will is from The Barn Bacon Company). There are regularly around 25 stalls with a huge range of produce.

Like everything else, the market has had to adapt to cope with Covid but is still a thriving place to come every Saturday.

Opposite: Thought to date from the 18th century, but possibly a little earlier, The Sun Inn was sometimes recorded as The Sun Coffee House. It's an unrivalled venue, with outdoor seating facing Barnes Pond, attracting customers from a wide area throughout the year, especially during the summer months.

Opposite, Bottom Right: Pre-covid and something that has just started to come back, on the first Saturday of every month from March, through to October, there is a lovely market by the pond.

Below: Hidden from view at the rear of The Sun Inn car park is a private bowling green. Beautifully maintained, unlike most clubs throughout the country, members play a unique form of bowls, where a pair of woods is used rather than four, play corner to corner and where the green is not flat.

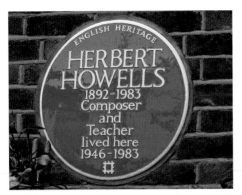

This Page, Below: The side view of one of four houses, Nos. 31–37 was once known locally as Atwell's Folly. Professor Henry Atwell, one time tutor to the Crown Prince of the Royal Dutch House of Orange-Nassau, ran a boarding school for boys in a house on the site from 1859, naming it Nassau House School. When he retired in 1890 the house was replaced by the four houses. They were built close to the road with basements, regarded by the locals as foolhardy in an area prone to flooding, hence the nickname. Nassau Road was laid out on the grounds of the school from which it took its name.

Top Left: In addition to the two plaques on The Terrace, there is also this to one of our finest composers (well I think so), Herbert Howells, that can be found behind the Green in Beverley Close.

Opposite: St Osmund's Catholic Primary School began as a convent school at the turn of the last century and St Osmund's took over in 1969. It's tucked behind the white house on Church Road (Opposite page top).

Back in 2019, and in conjunction with Sarah Arthur's Barnes Bugle (monthly newsletter, a must read for any resident), I was asked by Emma Robinson, our Town Centre Manager, to take some pictures of some of the notable local shop-keepers and with this new edition of my book, I felt it appropriate to feature some of them, especially given the torrid time that our high street has had just recently.

Opposite, Left to Right: Vipin from Natsons, Adam from &Feast and Malcom from Two Peas in a Pod.

This Page, Left: As I went to press on this new edition, our old Londis has gone through somewhat of a makeover, re-opening at the beginning of May 2021 as the Barnes Pantry; in need of any ingredient, you are sure to find it here

The Parish Church of St Mary, Barnes

The church dates from c.1100. A major fire on the 8th June 1978 left little standing. Fortunately, the south and east wall of the 12th/13th century chapel and the tower, C1485, survived to become an integral part of the rebuilt church designed by prize-winning architect Edward Cullinan. The re-hallowing of the new church took place on the 26th February 1984.

Top Right: The Homestead, Church Road. Built in the reign of Queen Anne (1702–1714) this attractive house with its old walled forecourt is one of the finest period houses remaining in Barnes. Seen together with its neighbours, St Mary's Church and Strawberry House, it presents a perfect picture of a bygone age.

Bottom: Strawberry House, Church Road. The former Barnes Rectory lost a substantial part of its land when Kitson Road, named after the rector, Benjamin Meredyth Kitson, was constructed in 1907. A further plot was used for the Church Hall in 1927, Kitson Hall (left). Built on the site of an earlier house, c.1717, it ceased to be the rectory in 1939 and stayed empty for some years until being finally sold in 1955, since when it has been a private residence. I am grateful to the current owner for allowing me to take a picture.

Right and Below: One of the new shops that has popped up in Barnes is Editor 37 in the old premises of the bookshop, that has moved down the street. What I love is that the new owner, Nikki, has retained the old bookshop sign and put it up on the wall in her shop.

This Page, Clockwise from the Left: More Barnes Heroes, Venetia from the Bookshop, Roger from Olympic Records, Azar from Blue Lavender, Natasha from Focalpoint and Camilla from Ridley.

Olympic Cinema and Restaurant/Byfield Hall, opened on 20th December 1906, was built on the site of a demolished private residence, Byfield House. The building was made up of two halls, one large and one small; the larger of the two could be hired for amateur theatricals, concerts or dances, the smaller for private events such as whist drives and parties. From 1910 until 1925 it operated as a cinema under a variety of names. Its most illustrious, albeit brief period, began in 1925 when Philip Ridgeway, a budding impressario, opened it as an art-house theatre. Famous names from the past, such as Charles Laughton, John Gielgud, Robert Newton and Claude Rains trod the boards in a series of productions, but a lack of funds resulted in its closure after barely a year, when it once again became a cinema.

In 1952 it became a studio for television commercials and later a recording studio where hits by The Beatles, The Rolling Stones, Pink Floyd, Led Zeppelin, Sting, U2 and many other leading groups were recorded. Having been sold by the beleaguered EMI, in October 2013 it opened as a wonderful new cinema and restaurant.

Top Left and Right: The Red Lion as it was a 100 years ago (with the entrance to the old Ranelagh Club, now Queen Elizabeth Walk) and as it is now. First recorded in 1718, when there was nothing to be seen to the north but farmland, this well-known pub was, at that time, a thatched hostelry known as *The Strugglers*. Destroyed by fire in 1835 it was rebuilt shortly after and re-named The Red Lion. During the 1880s it was a popular meeting place for the many cycling clubs in south west London who stopped for tea and a game at the skittle alley.

Barnes in Bloom

We live in a beautiful area, as these images amply demonstrate but did you know you can get involved? Each year, The Barnes Community Association (BCA) in the shape of their chairman, Nicki Urquhart, together with local sponsor Laurent Residential and a host of local volunteers go around each summer handing out awards for the best front gardens. So now you know.

Opposite, Clockwise from Top Left: The Sun Inn, St Mary's Church, Laurel Road and Barnes Common.

This Page, Top: North Barnes. **Clockwise from Top Left:** Church Road, Elm Grove Road (sad to hear that they have had to cut down some of these beautiful trees, the best road in Barnes for blossom for sure), The Olympic Cinema and The Crescent.

Ferry Road

As the name suggests, before the existence of Hammersmith Bridge, there used to be a ferry across the river to Chiswick and this was the route to it.

Towards the southern end you can find Walsingham Lodge. Set in three and a half acres of beautiful gardens between the Ferry and Berkeley Roads, right in the heart of Barnes, Walsingham Lodge is a development of 33 homes. Built in 1974 by what was then Barnes Workhouse Fund (now The Barnes Fund) on one half of the site of the old Barnes tennis club, Walsingham Lodge is a mix of almshouse flats and bungalows, and privately owned homes. On the other half of the same site is a residential care home Viera Gray House.

The High Street

This street of small shops and businesses at the heart of Barnes Village, is thought to have originated as the pathway between the two great open fields of medieval Barnes, the Northfield and the Westfield. It led from the village settlement around the Green to the river docking place, named as *le new docke* in 1400. A past local historian suggested that the pronounced bend in the High Street may have been trodden into being by the feet of men and draught animals having to avoid an immovable obstruction such as a large boulder or tree root in their path.

Below - Rose House: The Barnes Community Association was founded by its members over forty years ago. Then, as now, there were controversial changes proposed in Barnes which could affect the whole community. The founder members agreed that the BCA would channel opinion and influence decisions for the benefit of Barnes, and they raised funds to save Rose House, the 17th Century house, a former inn, from becoming a supermarket. It is now the BCA's headquarters and home.

Left to Right: More Barnes Heroes - Shamit from The Hardware Shop, Michael from the Fish Shop (did you know he's a Channel swimmer? No, nor did I until recently) and Valentina from The Cheese Shop.

"During the 45 years that I have lived in Barnes it has never occurred to me to go elsewhere.
It is leafy, it is attractive and it has shops which are so good, people from other areas visit them. It is wonderfully easy to get to the heart of London and out again. Every time I walk its streets I meet someone I know (and usually like!). It is cosy. Why would I want to move?"

JULIAN GLOVER, ACTOR, OCT 2011

Top: The High Street as it looked early last century. Thank you to the Barnes & Mortlake History Society for the use of this picture.

Bottom: The Coach & Horses pub in the High Street dates from the 18th century and is deceptively larger than you think, with a garden stretching far back from the road, including an excellent function room.

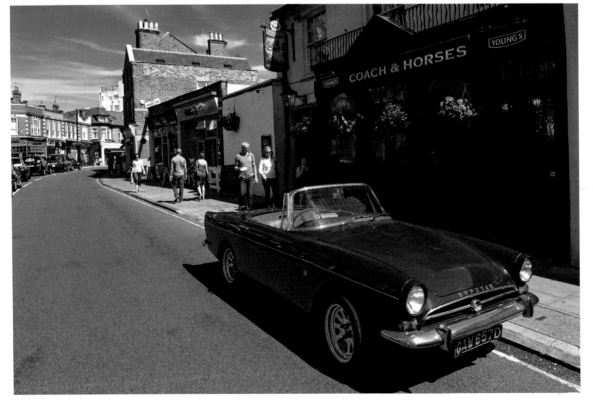

Top: Presents is one of the oldest shops in the High Street, 27 years prior to that it was two shops, a green grocer and an antique shop. That's the owner, Dharmesh, at the entrance.

Bottom: The Watermans Arms, on the corner of the High Street and Lonsdale Road, used to be a pub many years ago but more recently a series of restaurants; it was only when the last restaurant failed a couple of years ago, that an enterprising publican decided to reopen it as the pub that it always was.

Barnes in Lockdown

The first lockdown in 2020 resulted in a series of unusual sightings in Barnes, from huge lines of people at the only pub open in Barnes at the time, The Watermans, to guys on Penny Farthings enjoying the unseasonably good weather that we had, to multi coloured signs and streamers celebrating our wonderful NHS and public workers.

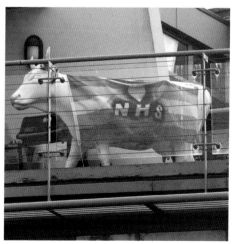

Rocks Lane

This Page: Rocks Lane is bordered on one side by a row of houses and on the other by a majestic line of plane trees and part of the Barn Elms Playing Fields.

Opposite: The Barnes base of the Rocks Lane family of sports centres is the oldest and recently celebrated their 25th birthday. The other clubs are in Chiswick and Bishop's Park in Fulham.

Station Road & Barnes Station

The Tudor-style brick-built station, opened on 27th July 1846 when the line to Richmond was built. It is the only survivor of others on the line built in the same style by Sir William Tite. Barnes became a junction station when the first section of the Hounslow Loop Line opened on the 22nd August 1849. The station and all lines serving it are today operated by South West Trains. The Grade II listed station house survives, but is now privately owned and no longer part of the railway.

Right: A painting of the station as it used to be in 1857; thank you to the Barnes & Mortlake History Society for the use of this image.

Opposite, Bottom Left and Right: In Station Road opposite the pond can be found the oldest surviving house in Barnes, Milbourne House, on the left next to Essex House. It assumed its present form in the 18th century, but the main building is probably sixteenth century. Only a public outcry prevented its demolition in 1945.

White Hart Lane
& West Barnes

Although officially in Mortlake, shops on the west side of White Hart Lane and such places as Rick Stein's in Mortlake High Street (opposite page top) are still very much part of the Barnes community.

Opposite, Bottom: Marianna out side her tea rooms, Orange Pekoe, and recently voted by the good people of Barnes as their favourite establishment.

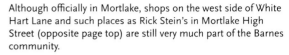

Ye White Hart

and the views west along the river

Starting out as the King's Arms, Ye White Hart changed its name in the 18th century. Rebuilt several times, the present large house dates from 1899. Always popular with rowers, the White Hart's commanding position on the riverside just above Barnes Bridge has for many years been a favourite viewing point for the Boat Race.

Opposite Top Right: One of the more significant changes to occur to White Hart Lane since my last edition has been the building of the footbridge over the railway line. Campaigned for over several years by local people, the bridge was finally opened in April 2019. A poll was taken running up to the opening for a name for the bridge and I rather like the winner, Hart Bypass.

Westfield Allotments

These allotments placed on undeveloped land between the railway and the pretty cottages in Railway Side are a rare survival from one of the two great open fields of Barnes, the Westfield. The allotment holders who tend their crops today, might sometimes give a thought to the Barnes peasants doing much the same in the early medieval period on the same plot of land. They might also think about the market garden labourers gathering the produce of the field for the London market from the 17th to the late 19th century.

Vine Road Recreation Ground

Vine Road Recreation Ground was in old times part of the large Westfield, then becoming an orchard before finally being turned into a park in the 1920s. Now administered by The Friends of Barnes Common, there are great plans in the pipeline for developing the park, with new amenities and the possible opening up of Beverley Brook, that runs alongside.

Hidden Barnes

This Page, Left: Beverley Brook as it glides between the houses on the roads behind Rocks Lane, Glebe Road, Bellevue Road, Rectory Road and Elm Grove Road. Elm Grove Road was laid on the site of Elm Grove – one of the lost houses of Barnes demolished in 1896. The house stood within the borders of the Barnes Elms estate near to where HSBC had their local bank, with grounds extending beyond the Beverley Brook to Barnes Common. It has been identified as the house occupied from 1703, by Jacob Tonson (1656–1736), who was a stationer, publisher and secretary to the Kit-Cat Club. Its members were the leading Whigs of the day, and are said to have met at the house with the purpose of promoting the House of Hanover and the Protestant Succession.

Below: The effigies on the houses are quite unique. The builder of these houses on the north side of Cedars Road finished them in 1901, which coincided with the ending of the Boer War and it is thought that he decided to date them by including two heroes from the war (Earl Kitchener and Earl Roberts) and Edward VII and his wife Queen Alexandra, top, as Edward became King that year.

Bottom Right: The Stormtrooper down Lonsdale Road.

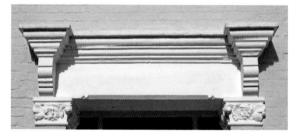

Top and Middle Left: Number 36 Railway Side, West Barnes, used to be a pub called The Beehive. Closed in the 80s, it was probably there to serve the labourers from the market gardens that used be here.

Top Middle: One of the old signs that can be found in the beer garden at The Brown Dog.

Top Right: The rather smart sign outside Barnes Atelier, the arts centre that can be found tucked behind the high street near Sainsburys.

Middle Right: The old entrance to Barnes Primary in Westfields Avenue.

Bottom Left: Back in the 70s, the famous singer, Marc Bolan, sadly died in a car crash on Queens Ride and his legion of fans had this commemorative stone put up.

Bottom Middle: Thorne Passage: This ancient track way ran due south-east across the Westfield as it does today, beginning at the junction of White Hart Lane and Barnes Terrace. In times past it provided a convenient dry route from Mortlake to Barnes when the river was in flood.

Bottom Right: This Skull can be found by the main door of St Mary's Church.

North Barnes

Over time, well the last 200 years certainly, North Barnes has been dominated by its relationship and proximity to Hammersmith Bridge, the gateway from Barnes to the rest of London. Sadly, as I prepare this latest edition of my book, with the Bridge's continued closure and with no end in sight, that relationship is brought into stark contrast. It might be quieter, good for the residents perhaps but with a huge drawback on connectivity.

That all being said, there are some lovely aspects to North Barnes, the bridge itself is still one of my favourites, to photograph at least, there is Barnes Waterside and Harrods Village, both with stunning views and what a place to live. The villas along Lonsdale Road and Castelnau and what a story there is to be found with the houses built by Henry Boot between the wars. Then of course, there is one of the best schools in the country. Let's hope for a quick resolution to the Bridge problem, even if it is in the first instance, just an opening up to pedestrians, as did indeed happen as we went to press (see below)

Castelnau over 100 years ago. Hammersmith Bridge. As we went to press on this latest edition, the bridge suddenly reopened to foot passengers, which was amazing news for the people of Barnes. Before this welcome news there was talk of a ferry being set-up with large pontoons out into the river to take account of the tides. It is interesting to note that back in 1906 there was something similar at the foot of one of the pillars.

North Barnes

Opposite: Castelnau Villas. After opening the first Hammersmith Bridge in 1827, it was some time before the first of the ribbon development of houses began to replace the market gardens and farmlands stretching back from the newly built approach road, Upper Bridge Road (now Castelnau). Castelnau Villas were the first to be built in 1842, six years into the reign of Queen Victoria. The architect was Harry Laxton. Originally unnumbered, they are now Nos. 84–122 and 91–125 Castelnau.

This Page: Castelnau

Bottom Left: Barnes local library, half way down Castelnau.

Opposite: St Osmund's Church, the first purpose built Roman Catholic Church in Barnes, opened in 1954. From the end of the 19th century, mass had been ministered by a priest from Mortlake in the chapel of a girls' school in Church Road, Barnes which later became part of St. Osmund's R.C. School. In 1908 the congregation bought No.77 Castelnau, which served as a temporary chapel and housing for the Priest. This later became the site for the present church, the opening being much delayed by WW2. No. 79 seen to the right of the church is the Presbytery or Priest's House.

This Page: Holy Trinity Church, Castelnau, built in 1868 on the east side of Upper Bridge Road (re-named Castelnau, 1889). Holy Trinity replaced an earlier chapel-of-ease built in 1851 for the growing community in North Barnes. Originally served by clergy from St. Mary's Parish Church, Holy Trinity became a separate parish in 1880. The architect, Thomas Allom, lived in Lonsdale Road.

Opposite – Castelnau Estate: This pleasant well-laid out cottage style estate of 640 ferro-concrete houses was built in 1926 to ease the over crowded conditions in Hammersmith and Fulham. It was built on Harold Bessant's market garden land by Henry Boot & Sons by a method known as the Boot Pier and Panel System. During the late '70s several tenants bought their homes under the Central Government's 'right to buy scheme'. In November 1983 reports that identical Boot Houses in other parts of the country had been declared structurally unsound, resulted in several owner-occupied homes on Castelnau Estate being virtually rebuilt in conventional red brick. It was later found that all but one of the houses on the estate were in fact perfectly sound.

This Page: Castelnau Recreation Ground is tucked away behind Washington Road and Barnes Avenue and is a great open space. The Council consulted the residents regarding the gate and the result is rather magnificent.

This Page: With the development of the Castelnau Estate in 1926, there was a need for a new school and within three years Lowther Primary started in Stillingfleet Road. They have a magnificent main building, which reflects the age it was built in and since the main picture was taken they have added another building to the school (see bottom left). They have a lot of space and put it to good use, with an allotment and even some chickens.

Opposite and Overleaf: The present Hammersmith Bridge, designed by Sir Joseph William Bazalgette, was opened by Prince Albert Victor of Wales on Saturday 18th June 1887. It replaced an earlier bridge, designed by William Tierney Clark (see page 8) and opened without ceremony in October 1827. By 1877 the narrow width of Tierney Clark's bridge and its safety under increasingly heavy traffic was in question and in 1882 the bridge committee voted in favour of a new bridge. A temporary bridge was erected on clusters of timber piles close to the western side of the old bridge during the period of demolition and construction. This may all sound very 2021, for as we go to press on this new edition, the fate of the bridge is in a state of flux due to its closure on safety grounds. The cost of putting it right is quite prohibitive for the local council to manage on their own. As we go to press, after 18 months of closure, the bridge is only just re-opening to pedestrians.

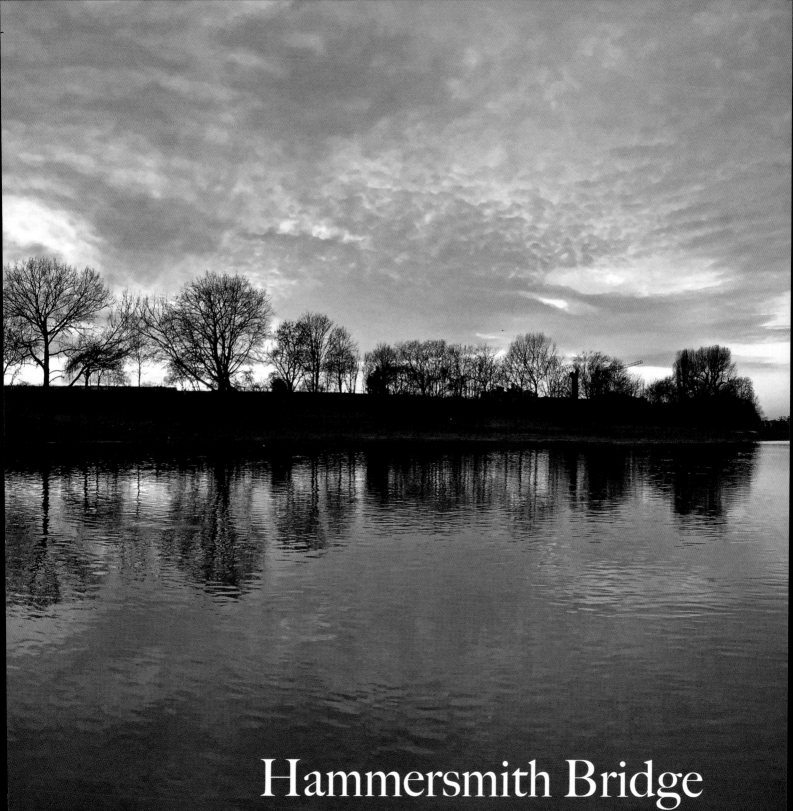

Hammersmith Bridge

Barn Elms Allotments, found beside Barnes Riverside, has to be one of the smartest looking allotments you'll find; it has manicured grass pathways between each plot and it has its own highway with a speed limit. It is home to some lovely people, who obviously care passionately about what they do.

Top left: Lynda and her wonderful hat.

Bottom left: Queenie and Hayley – they even had the smartest looking shed you'll ever see too!

Harrods Village & Barnes Waterside

Top Left: The temple and fountain that greets visitors to Harrods Village.

Top Right: The rather impressive viewing deck beside the pond in Barnes Waterside.

Centre: The very distinctive apartment blocks within Barnes Waterside.

Bottom: Harrods Depository from the river.

Opposite: The very attractive pond within Barnes Waterside.

St Paul's School & Colet Court

The famous public school for boys was founded in 1509 by the Dean of St Paul's Cathedral, John Colet. In 1884 it moved from its original site near the Cathedral to West Kensington where it remained until, together with its preparatory school, Colet Court, it moved to Barnes in 1968. The new school with sports grounds and a boathouse by the Thames was purpose built on a disused reservoir site.

This Page, Top: An example of the impressive villas to be found along the top of Lonsdale Road as it nears Hammersmith Bridge.

This Page, Bottom: Castelnau Community Centre can be found in Stillingfleet Road and its aim is to provide a vibrant, self-sustaining community for the Castelnau estate and the surrounding area. It came very much to the fore during the recent pandemic by providing food parcels and other essential help for the residents of Barnes.

Opposite: The Swedish School was founded in 1907 in Harcourt Street, Central London. The lower school moved to Lonsdale Road, Barnes in 1976.

Harrodian School

An independent pre-prep and preparatory school for boys and girls opened in 1993 in Lonsdale Road. Originally occupying the former house and sports club belonging to the department store, Harrods of Knightsbridge, it has since been considerably enlarged and currently has around 900 pupils.

Left: Barnes Sports Club, which can be found opposite Small Profit Dock on Lonsdale Road. Besides cricket, amongst the other sports played are tennis and squash.

This Page, Bottom and Opposite: Small Profit Dock is the name that has been given to the small triangular stretch of land off Lonsdale Road and opposite Gerard and Nassau Roads. The actual dock is the curved railing on the embankment by the river. The parking bay at Small Profit Dock has been renovated since this picture was taken. The picture at the top of the page is of ring-necked parakeets fighting over the hole in the tree that can be found in the centre of the dock.

Barnes Common
and other open spaces

Sometimes we overlook the things that are on our doorstep. Hidden gems like Barnes Common or Leg o' Mutton Reservoir can offer us as much as the great moors and national parks if, like your author Andrew, you are prepared to invest a little time in understanding them. They can offer just as much inspiration, calm for reflection and opportunity to appreciate the wonders of Nature. Sometimes what we observe is special – a rare bird, reptile or butterfly. Other times it is a sight, a sound, the feel of the breeze, the scent of rain or soil, the first flowers of Spring or trees in bud, clouds, sunshine, maybe a small creature or plant surviving against the odds...

When mankind is consuming the world's resources at an estimated 1.6 times natural recovery rates, and as we emerge from a pandemic that has shocked us into recognising how fragile man's place is on this planet. We all need to raise not only our awareness of the dangers of climate change and the need to change lifelong habits of consumption, but also our appreciation of the wonders of the natural world and the incredible miracle that is life.

Better appreciation of Nature is a good place to start....and if you want to appreciate Nature more, what better introduction than this book?

Andrew's wonderful photographs chronicle his own engagement with Nature on his own doorstep; this book offers us all a chance of greater appreciation through his dedication, artistic creativity, mastery of composition and light, as well as patience to be in the right place at the right time.

My hope is that you will be inspired to explore more for yourself; and that you will join us in looking after this very special place, which some of us are so fortunate to be able to call our home.

Mike Hildesley
Chair, Friends of Barnes Common,
Barnes, June 2021.

The junction at Mill Hill as it is today and over 100 years ago.

Winter

It doesn't snow that often but when it does, the common can look beautiful.

This Page, Top: The fabulous goldcrest, the UK's smallest bird, can be found on the common and easier to spot in winter when there are no leaves to obstruct your view.

Opposite, Bottom: The Grand Old Oak on the common, to be found in the woods near Vine Road.

Top Left: Yellow brain fungus. **Top Right:** Kestrel. **Bottom:** Sunrise over The Orchard. **Opposite:** A fox in The Orchard

Spring
Blackthorn & Blossom

With the onset of March comes the first signs of spring on the common, blossom and the early butterflies, orange tips (Middle bottom) and peacocks (opposite bottom left). Birds also start to sing for a mate, the wonderful chiffchaff (below bottom right).

Green, Blue & Gold
Grasses & Acid Grassland

Green alkanet might be considered a menace by gardeners but is an early feast for insects seeking nectar.

Below Left: A bumble bee.

Bottom Left: A bee fly.

Below Right: Bluebells.

Bottom Right: The green hairstreak, which likes gorse.

We have almost 30 grasses on the common and the Friends of Barnes Common are currently cataloguing them and hope to have them up on their website come the autumn of 2021 – www.barnescommon.or.uk

Lowland Acid Grassland is rare across London and The South East due to amongst other things, over development. We are lucky to have quite a bit on Barnes Common and work feverishly to preserve it. Characterised by such plants as cats ears and sheep's sorrel (below bottom), which carpet the common in late spring and early summer.

With spring come many nesting animals to the common.

This Page, Top: A young treecreeper.

Bottom: Mating damselfies.

Opposite, Top: Tawny owlets.

Bottom, Left to Right: Nuthatch, fox cub and great spotted woodpecker.

Long Hot Days of Summer

We share the common with the community, whether they be cricketers or dog walkers.

Top Left: One of the new benches on the common, the Iris bench.

Right: Essex skipper butterfly.

Down by the Brook

We regularly trawl Beverley Brook to check for life.

Bringing in the Hay

When the weather is set fine in late August or early September, we cut the meadows for hay and for the first time in 2020, we donated our hay to a stables in Richmond.

It's a Small World

This Page, Clockwise from Top Left: Dock bug, ladybird, garden spider, female thick-legged beetle (they don't have the thick legs apparently), common darter and the majestic wasp-spider.

Opposite, Top: Painted lady butterfly.

Bottom from the Left: Marbled white butterfly, meadow brown butterfly being devoured by a crab spider and the bee wolf.

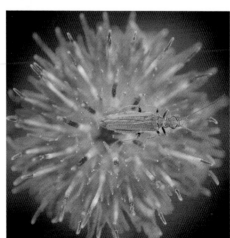

Autumn

Below and Right: Maisie's Meadow, which you reach via the small bridge over the brook from Barnes Green.

Bottom: A rare sight these days, a hedgehog, especially in daylight. Thanks to a local resident, Michel Birkenwald, a lot of work has been done to make our gardens hog-friendly.

The common in autumn is a wonderful place to discover all types of fungi.

Clockwise from the Left: Fly agaric, mycena, chanterelle, wood ears, sulfur tufts with the robin, inkcaps and golden scalycap.

As the days shorten, October can still provide a little warmth on the common, and there are still one or two butterflies on the wing.

Below Left: The last common blue

Right: The last small copper.

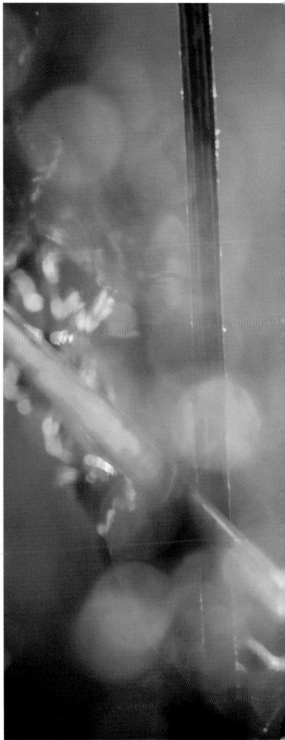

Leg o' Mutton
Nature Reserve
Winter

In the 60s a disused reservoir along Lonsdale Road was saved from development by the actions of some locals (please see picture below for what it looked like back then). It has since become a nature reserve, a haven for wildlife and is now in the care of The Friends of Barnes Common.

Leg o' Mutton
Nature Reserve
Spring & Summer

This Page, Clockwise from Top Left: Reed warbler, local artist, heron chicks, tawny owlets and the parent (tiring work, as all parents would identify with).

Opposite, Clockwise from Top Left: Young squirrels, cygnets, blue tit amongst the reeds and cygnets from 2020.

Above: Kestrel nest, mallard ducklings. **Right:** The drought of 2019, where the water level got very low.

Leg o' Mutton
Nature Reserve
Autumn

The colour in autumn can be spectacular, mainly down to the maple, which being non-native, is being cut back as too invasive.

Below: The team from The Friends of Barnes Common doing some tree work.

Barn Elms

The Old Cemetery, Barnes Common

Known today as Barnes Old Cemetery or Rocks Lane Cemetery, this small burial ground on 2 acres of land within Barnes Common, opened in 1854, shortly after the churchyard of the Parish Church of St Mary was closed for burials. Some 3,000 burials took place here, the majority being of local people, before it was declared full and closed in the mid-1950s. Since its closure the majority of the gravestones have been vandalised, lending an air of dereliction to the once pleasant surroundings. Recent efforts by the Friends of Barnes Common have vastly improved the general ambiance and in 1980 the Managers, Richmond Council, succeeded in having the Cemetery declared a Local Nature Reserve.

MAJOR
G. BUDIBENT
ARMY SERVICE CORPS
2ND OCTOBER 1918

WWT London Wetland Centre
Winter

In the same way that the Leg o' Mutton Reservoir was saved from being developed, so was The London Wetland Centre. Starting out as four reservoirs (pictured left), by the 1970s they had become redundant and Thames Water were looking to move them on. Up step Sir Peter Scott (the vision), Gyles Brandreth (the local man on the ground) and Tony Pidgley from The Berkeley Group (the money), who approach Thames Water with a breath taking scheme to completely revolutionise the area to what it is today. See my new book Wild about Wetlands (out for Christmas 2021) for the full story.

Below Right: the fabulous Lapwing.

Bottom Left: The winter visitor you may hear before you can see them, the booming bittern.

WWT London Wetland Centre

Spring

This Page, Clockwise from Top Right: Barnacle goose, Bewick swan, reed warbler and great crested grebe.

"When I came to live here 25 years ago, on behalf of the Barn Elms Protection Association I went to visit Sir Peter Scott at Slimbridge on the Severn Estuary to discuss the idea of bringing a wildfowl and wetlands to Barn Elms. He leapt at the idea and told me, 'If the birds like it in Barnes they'll come. If they really like it, they'll come again and again.' Birds are fine judges of a place. The London Wetland Centre is now the finest urban wildlife site in Europe. The Berwick swans have spoken. Enough said."

GYLES BRANDRETH, AUTUMN 2011

Top: Mute swan. **Bottom:** Canada goose.

WWT London Wetland Centre

Summer

This Page, Top Left: Moorhen nest.

Right: Asian short-clawed otter.

Bottom: White-faced whistling ducks.

Opposite, Top left: Lapwing.

Opposite, Right: The Peacock Tower.

Opposite, Bottom: Gatekeeper butterfly amongst the wild flowers.

WWT London Wetland Centre
Autumn

Opposite, Top Left: Emperor goose.

Opposite, Top Right: Kingfisher.